T0040291

EVERY DAY SHOULD BE

# FATHER'S DAY

EVERY DAY SHOULD BE

# FATHER'S
# DAY

## 50 Ways to Honor, Appreciate, Indulge, and Amuse Your Dad

Jennifer Basye Sander

with Cathy MacHold

Skyhorse Publishing

Skyhorse Publishing books may be purchased in bulk at special discounts for sales promotion, corporate gifts, fund-raising, or educational purposes. Special editions can also be created to specifications. For details, contact the Special Sales Department, Skyhorse Publishing, 307 West 36th Street, 11th Floor, New York, NY 10018 or info@skyhorsepublishing.com.

Skyhorse® and Skyhorse Publishing® are registered trademarks of Skyhorse Publishing, Inc.®, a Delaware corporation.

Visit our website at www.skyhorsepublishing.com.

10 9 8 7 6 5 4 3 2 1

Library of Congress Cataloging-in-Publication Data is available on file.

Cover design by Laura Klynstra
Cover image by gettyimages

Print ISBN: 978-1-5107-5235-1
Ebook ISBN: 978-1-5107-5236-8

Printed in China

# INTRODUCTION

In past decades and generations, fathers tended to be viewed as these unknowable creatures of mystery, slipping out of the house in the morning for the office and then returning glumly at the end of the day, retreating into their study with a cigarette, the newspaper, and a glass of scotch. But now, fathers are thankfully much more visible in everyday life, and they are happy to be stay-at-home dads or breadwinners. Therefore, the old method of buying a bottle of aftershave and a tie that reigned supreme in the 50s and 60s as a standard Father's Day gift is delightfully out of date.

Is spending time with your dad any different than spending time with a friend? Yes, and no. Some of your fathers may be young, some may be getting up there in years . . . so although we tried to keep the age range in mind while offering up these suggestions, some might work better than others for the dad in your life. We've tried to offer up ideas for all price ranges and budgets, from completely free to what the heck, let's blow the doors off your (or your dad's) bank account. And wherever possible we provide ideas on how to do these things for all ages and physical abilities.

There are many ways that we can celebrate beyond the giving of commercial gifts and we can do it every day in meaningful ways. Establishing new traditions or following old ones, showing gratitude with love and affection goes beyond a funny coffee mug or a funny T-shirt. This is a book about sharing experiences and building the bond between father and child. In a broader sense, you could share these ideas with an uncle, a brother, or maybe someone who hasn't experience fatherhood yet. This collection of compelling ideas will take you from sporty adventures to shared culinary experiences, and you don't have to be a millionaire to do them.

Where do these ideas come from? In our modern world, ideas are constantly flashed before us with imagery through media or movies or from any of our devices. We can move away from the sidelines and participate in shared activities a lot easier than you might think. There are more resources and opportunities now than ever before. It requires creativity and imagination—and, we might add, some planning. It's easy to become part of those dreams using your time and energy. You'll find ways in this book to re-purpose old things making them new again. You'll discover that it doesn't require a lot of money for you to share lasting and loving memorable experiences with your father every day.

We hope this collection of ideas and suggestions will move you emotionally, lovingly, physically, and meaningfully to create more shared experiences with the father in your life.

A Note to Dads: Happy Father's Day! If you received this book as a gift, think of it as a smorgasbord of ideas that you can urge your kids to do with you! In fact, why not mark it up: circle the things that interest you the most, cross out the ideas that don't appeal, and then give the book back to them so they can start planning an outing or two?

# BREWING CLASS

The US seems like one big brew pub sometimes, with a new rustic onsite brewery opening in every town each weekend. There is no shortage of places to drink bespoke beer. Has the popularity of small batch brewing inspired you to give it a try on your own? Or maybe it's cider that intrigues you? Why not ask your dad if he also has an interest in trying to become a home brewer?

Check out home brewing classes at adult education venues near you like public libraries or community colleges. You could also join the American Homebrewers Association and learn from their online tutorials and forums: homebrewersassociation.org. A one-year membership is currently less than $50 and gives you access to everything you need to get started.

According to beverage industry studies, although beer volume declined for five years straight, US residents consumed 26.5 gallons of beer and cider per person in 2018.

# WILD NIGHT IN

**W**hile the food world is all agog about plant-based meat like the Impossible Burger, your dad might be more interested in going wild at this point in his life. Wild game, that is. If your family doesn't hunt (or know someone who does and is willing to share the bounty) there are many sources for ordering wild game and having it delivered for a special dinner. Check out Cavendish Game Birds of Vermont at cavendishgamebirds.com, or check out the offerings of free-range venison, antelope, or wild boar at Texas's Broken Arrow Ranch, brokenarrowranch. com.

Hunting as an activity is falling off in many states, but maybe you and your father could take a hunter safety class together. There are now online courses you can take in the comfort of your own home, and even if you never plan to hunt, it's a good thing to know how to safely handle guns.

Looking for recipes on what to do with your wild game? Cookbook author and dedicated hunter Hank Shaw runs a great site called Honest-Food.net that is filled with delicious advice. His blog, *Hunter, Angler, Gardner, Cook*, is well worth following if you want to have a more direct relationship with your food.

"I love the comic opportunities that come up in the context of a father-son relationship."

–Harrison Ford

# COMMUNITY CLEAN-UP

**N**o need to butt heads with your elders over who believes what about climate change; why not instead find a community clean-up day nearby and pick up your own little corner of the world together? Your local parks, neighborhoods, and business districts could all use a little help, and pitching in on an organized clean-up is a great way to give back. Working side by side with your father to pick up trash might well spark him to share memories of times past in the park or neighborhood or what businesses used to be where back in the day. Keep your eyes peeled for info on a local clean-up effort, or check out kab.org, the website of Keep America Beautiful, and search for an event near you.

Can't find one in your area? Why not organize one for your own community? Budgetdumpster.com has a list of tips for planning a clean-up day, from choosing a focus to recruiting volunteers and even throwing the post-clean-up party.

> Your dad might remember when, in 1965, the First Lady of the United States, Lady Bird Johnson, joined the Keep America Beautiful campaign to beautify the nation's highways, or, in 1967, Lassie appeared as a mascot for an anti-litter campaign.

# DOG SLEDDING

Alaska is on many a bucket list, and what could be more adventurous than standing behind a team of hardworking dogs pulling a sled through the snow? The childhood dream of any boy who read a Jack London story comes to life! Every so often it's fun to daydream about a big ticket item, and heading to Alaska for a dogsledding trip with your father certainly fits the bill. Check out the dream trips on Yukonwild.com

Down in the Lower 48, there are also opportunities to ride behind a team of dogs. In California, you can experience an afternoon trip near Lake Tahoe with Sierra Adventures, info at wildsierra.com. In Colorado, there are several companies that operate near ski resorts like Steamboat Springs and Breckenridge. The state tourism site, Colorado.com, has a complete list to peruse. Minnesota has a thriving dog sledding community also, information at dogsledding.com.

# Unforgettable Father Moments

I'd just finished intelligence school in Baltimore and was sent to Washington, DC, on special assignment before my tour in Vietnam. On a two-week leave, the plan was to meet my dad on the freeway outside of DC. It was hot and sunny that day. My dad was driving a semi-truck from New York to Florida—we'd arranged to meet at a specified offramp on the interstate at a certain time. I was standing at the agreed location waiting for my dad when I saw him drive by without stopping, without even looking. My heart raced. *He drove right by*, I thought. "No, oh no." I looked around. *He didn't even look*, I thought. It all seemed to happen in slow motion. I started waiving frantically thinking we were going to miss each other. *Was that it?* I hoped not.

Luckily, a trucker who was following my dad noticed that something was amiss. He radioed him thinking he knew what had just happened. I felt a huge sense of relief as my dad circled back, finally picking me up. We then drove to Florida sharing driving duties, which I greatly enjoyed, having never driven a semi-truck before. As both of us relaxed from the near miss, we began a great conversation. We hadn't seen each other in four years and had a lot to catch up about. My dad was able to share his experiences from WWII. He helped prepare me for what I was about to experience myself in Vietnam. This was the first time that I was really able to bond with my dad having that "man to man" conversation. I had a great week in Florida with him before returning to California, then on to Vietnam. That visit with my dad will live in my heart always.

—Ken MacHold

# KEEP ON BOOKING

Ask any bookseller, and they will tell you that the run up to Father's Day is one of the biggest book-buying seasons of the year. And who knows what people read better than librarians? So of course we asked booksellers and librarians for their ideas on great books for dads:

"Anything by David McCullough," was the answer we got from one long-time bookseller. McCullough has written on topics as varied as the building of the Brooklyn Bridge and the Wright Brothers to various US presidents and most recently, *The Pioneers: The Heroic Story of the Settlers Who Brought the American Ideal West.* Other gift worthy book ideas for dads include:

> *The British are Coming: The War for America, Lexington to Princeton, 1775-1777*, by Rick Atkinson
>
> *The Boys in the Boat: Nine Americans and Their Epic Quest for Gold at the 1936 Berlin Olympics*, by Daniel James Brown
>
> *George Washington's Secret Six: The Spy Ring that Saved the American Revolution*, by Brian Kilmeade and Don Yaeger
>
> *A Walk in the Woods: Rediscovering America on the Appalachian Trail*, by Bill Bryson

*Lost Founding Father: John Quincy Adams and the Transformation of American Politics*, by William J. Cooper

*Big Russ & Me: Father & Son: Lessons of Life,* by Tim Russert

"The older I get, the smarter my father seems to get," Tim Russert wrote. "Hardly a day goes by when I don't remember something that Big Russ taught me." Maybe reading Russert's book will inspire you to write up a few of the things that you learned from your own father.

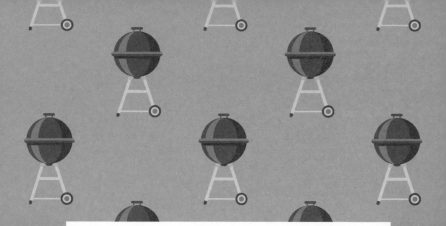

"The greatest mark of a father is how he treats his children when no one is looking."

–Dan Pearce

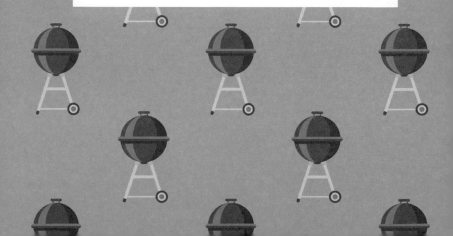

# VINTAGE HUNTING

**H**as your father ever waxed nostalgic about the car he was desperate to own in high school? Something a neighbor or maybe the football star owned? Or perhaps there was a watch that he loved but one day lost and still mourns?

Why not arrange a date with your dad to go on the hunt for vintage treasures? You could spend an afternoon in a u-pull-it yard or a junkyard, walking among the rusted hulks of cars he remembers clearly, or visit a car museum to hear him share memories. Thrift stores, consignment shops, and even yard sales in every town are filled with items that could spur nostalgic moments and perhaps inspire a purchase. Just don't hurt his feelings and suggest a trip to an "antique store" to look for childhood possessions. "Vintage" is a much softer word!

Maybe what you and your father need is a visit to what is billed as "The World's Largest Garage Sale." The town of Warrensburg, New York, has been hosting the yearly event in October for more than forty years, and it is described as a combination of a flea market, craft fair, food fest, and bargain hunter's dream. Could be an item for your bucket list . . . warrensburgchamber.com

# Unforgettable Father Moments

My father was born in and lived in the Kingdom of Romania. By the time I was born in 1974 and following the changes that World War II brought, Romania became the Romania's People's Republic, a communist country. I remember standing in line for everything as a child, hoping to get a chicken, bread, butter, even flour. Dad would leave for work. My brother and I had the job of holding our place in line with other families. The line got longer as the day progressed. Brother first, for an hour, then it was my turn. I'd stand for another hour then my brother and I would switch. We leap frogged the hours away until 4:00 p.m. when Dad came and we'd stand in line all together; Mom too.

More and more people arrived as the hours passed. It was common practice for the kids to mark a place in line for the family. As an adult in the modern world, and now in the US, I find it very hard to want to stand in any line, but now my kids want to visit Disneyland. I actually have nightmares about standing in line. But I love my kids, and I want them to have the experiences in life that brighten the spirit and create a better memory.

Recently my oldest son told me that Disneyland added a new bathroom pass. It allows riders to leave the line, head to

the bathroom and then re-enter through the Fast Pass line where they wait in a holding area where the rest of the family waits. My son thought this "selling point" would convince me that standing in line for the Disney California Adventure Park would be fun. How could I turn down this opportunity for my sons to stand in line with Dad? After all, it's at the front of the line where all the fun begins, right? I used it as an opportunity to tell my kids about my life and their grandfather's life in what was once another Kingdom, but not near as much fun as in the Magic Kingdom.

—Sergio Chirila

# BOARD ROOM

**D**id your father harbor a secret (or maybe not-so-secret) desire to surf in his youth? Or maybe he is now looking with envy at paddle boarders gliding on the lake surface. Could be a kayak is more his speed, but whatever his water-borne dream, you can take steps to bring it alive.

Kayak and SUP (stand up paddleboard) rental companies abound near watery places, and if there is a surf break nearby then there is a surf school nearby. No need to undergo a lengthy commitment, just a one-day quick lesson and board rental will do the trick and give you (yes, you'd better get out there on the board or in the kayak too) both a taste of the boarding life.

Kayaking might be easier for dads who have knee issues and can't balance on a paddleboard.

An afternoon of water sports sounds like a fine way to bond as a family, but on occasion an element of competition can creep in . . . Camille Hayes remembers a family kayak afternoon that, as she described it, "Was far from a touching bonding moment. It devolved into a race which my dad claimed to have won, even though my husband Drew was towing him most of the way." Ah well, maybe next time it will be more touching.

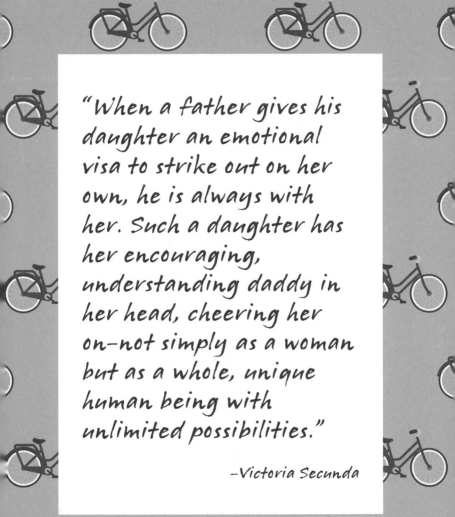

"When a father gives his daughter an emotional visa to strike out on her own, he is always with her. Such a daughter has her encouraging, understanding daddy in her head, cheering her on—not simply as a woman but as a whole, unique human being with unlimited possibilities."

–Victoria Secunda

# GIVE A GO BAG

**N**atural disaster stories fill our news feed daily, from hurricanes and floods to earthquakes and fires. These disasters are top of mind for you, and you might have already gathered up a small store of emergency supplies and made a family disaster plan. But what about your folks? Is your dad good to go in an emergency? You can help your dad put together a basic "go bag" by making sure that he has the following on hand:

- Water—one gallon per person for three days

- Food—a three-day supply of non-perishables

- Batteries—all sizes should be kept on hand; check to see what your flashlights and other equipment require

- Flashlights with fresh batteries

- Hand cranked radio and phone charger

With older parents it is also recommended to have an extra supply of prescription medicines on hand should pharmacies not be accessible during an emergency. Are either of your parents on medical devices that require electricity? In a disaster how will that be handled? Better to ask now and take steps to be prepared than have to scramble when disaster strikes. Check out the list of supplies suggested by Redcross.com and help your father start to build up what would be needed for a few days.

Have you taken a CPR or emergency medicine class lately? Maybe now is the time, and perhaps your father will sign up and take it alongside. Any emergency training is helpful in making you better able to handle whatever might happen in life.

# Unforgettable Father Moments

My father is present with me always. In my childhood, I could not understand the reasons for his stern, authoritative discipline, and, like many children, I learned quickly to ask Mom when Pop would say "No." As the years progressed, the man who had been a professor of Romanticism in German literature would detail our family's fabled history across continents and eras with a wistful expression, a nostalgia for times past. This, along with a world classical music he would play at the piano or on phonograph records, enriched my childhood.

My father, Antonio Carlos Bombal v. Hagel was born in Chile in 1932 and met my mother Judy Stocking in 1966, when she was an exchange student visiting the South American country. They were a bright and intelligent couple. I came along in 1967, also in Chile, where mom started to get homesick for the US. Out of love for his wife, my father pulled up his Chilean roots and came to live with her—opposites attract. By the time I was seventeen, my father's old country ways and conservative aristocratic attitudes were too much for my dear mother, a liberal-minded, live-and-let-live type with an indestructible work ethic. They separated, and I began sharing time with my parents in two different places rather than our single-family home.

At this point a curious change occurred—our traditional father-son relationship morphed into a great friendship; we became the best of pals until he died in 2009. The death of a parent remains tough for the rest of our own days. In loving reflection, memories persist; my childhood trip to Brooks Brothers, San Francisco, to be measured for long trousers, with a yearly trip thereafter for a new blue blazer, Pop making sure that I had natural shoulders in the jackets. A trip to the Campanile on the UC Berkeley campus where the mechanics of the bells fascinated me until their peal was so loud I ran screaming in fear. On another visit there in the library stacks, Pop saved me from tear gas pouring out of the vents during a student protest in the early 1970s by hiding my face under his Harris tweed jacket as we fled. His precise instruction on the making of a Pisco Sour cocktail, a matter of national pride, was effectively learned and is still practiced to the present day. Countless moments flood my memory, but his deathbed advice I treasure: "When you shake someone's hand, put your heart in it."

—Matias Bombal

# SHARPEN KNIVES AND TOOLS

**S**mall gestures of kindness and concern are meaningful, even if they seem so everyday and ordinary. Take a look in the kitchen where your father lives—are things looking a little on the dull side? And what about the garage; is his chainsaw chain looking a bit rusty? Lawnmower need to be serviced? Barbecue need a new propane tank? Here is your chance to gather a few things up and take them to be sharpened and serviced. Even if they are seldom used at this point in your dad's life, keeping them combat ready is a way of telling your father that you know he is still the same guy he used to be when he was mowing the lawn every Saturday and grilling up some steaks later that night. And then, of course, they will be operational if and when you step in and take over the tasks.

Even if your father has lost interest in mowing the lawn or gardening, he still needs to get outside for his health. Being outside increases your exposure to vitamin D, which is critical (in limited dosages) for maintaining bone strength.

"In wisdom gathered over time, I have found that every experience is a form of exploration."

—Ansel Adams

# MOVING ONLINE

How tech savvy is your dad? Does he need your help in maintaining an online presence? Maybe he has a small business that needs some online marketing. Maybe he is a late-stage career man who needs help with creating a LinkedIn account or sprucing up his resume for a career change. And if your dad is single at this point in his life, maybe he needs help with Match.com or eHarmony. Or . . . maybe you can find someone else to help him with that task if it makes you feel a bit squeamish.

Ride sharing apps are a great way for seniors to cut back on their own driving and let someone else get them where they need to go. Does your dad need help loading an app like Uber or Lyft onto his phone? Or if he doesn't feel comfortable with that, check out gogograndparent.com, which lets seniors make a phone call to a central dispatch who will then communicate with the ride sharing service. It doesn't require a smartphone and might be easier for some older dads.

There are also dating sites that cater to seniors. The dating apps OurTime, Stitch, SeniorMatch, and Senior PeopleMeet all have minimum age requirements. If your dad is over the half century mark, these might be the ones to steer him toward, should he ask for your advice about dating.

# TIED IN KNOTS

Of course you know how to tie a knot. We all need knots in our lives; good solid knots are required for boating, camping, gardening, and various household tasks. But when was the last time you sat down and tried to learn a new knot? Now is a good time to try, and perhaps your father can teach you. Was he a Boy Scout in his early years? They're required to learn a variety of knots—ask him if he remembers a few and can teach them to you. He might enjoy showing off what he can remember, and it could also be a fun activity with his grandchildren.

Knots require dexterity, so get those fingers going. If your father doesn't have a knot or two to teach you, look for knot tying videos online and try to learn a new one together. Netknots.com is a good place to start learning to tie one.

Hand dexterity is an important thing to hang on to as we age. Even squeezing small ball while watching TV, or making a fist a few times a day can help keep fingers nimble. Encourage your father to keep moving those digits.

# THEIR FARM TO YOUR FORK

**A**nytime is a good time to get outside and enjoy the fresh air, even better if you are outside loading up on fresh fruits and vegetables. Do you have childhood memories of a day on a farm with your family, visiting relatives and picking a few things out of the field? No doubt your father has similar memories, even if it was only once or twice a year.

You might already have a family tradition of picking out your own pumpkin or cutting down your own Christmas tree, but why not extend that great family outing throughout the year? All across the country there are farms and orchards that encourage customers to come and pick their own bounty. From Angelic Gardens in Minot, North Dakota, to Phelps Fruit & Berry Farm in Payson, Utah, Braeutigam Orchards in Belleville, Illinois, and all points beyond, visit Upickfarmlocator. com to find a place near you.

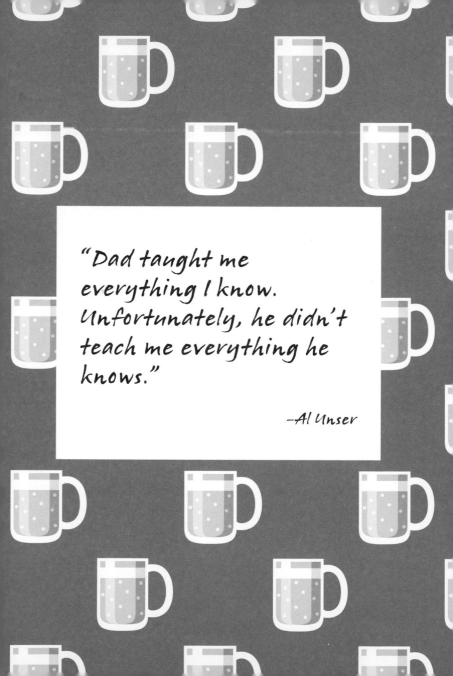

"Dad taught me everything I know. Unfortunately, he didn't teach me everything he knows."

—Al Unser

# Unforgettable Father Moments

[Overture fades; single spot comes up on a young boy]

Teenage Boy: [acapella] One day I will be an actor. One day I will stand on a great stage and take my curtain call to the applause of thousands.

[Fade to black]

[Curtain rises on San Francisco street. Middle-aged man hurrying nine-year-old boy across the stage].

Father: [recitative] Hurry, hurry. We are late for the auditions. Hurry.

Son: I don't want to audition. I don't want to be an extra in an opera. Just because you wanted to be an actor and never were, doesn't mean I have to audition with you!

Father: Well you have to come with me. You may as well just do the audition instead of standing around. You probably won't even get picked. If you do, you can say "no thanks."

[Fade to black]

So began our foray into the world of the San Francisco Opera Supernumeraries. The SF Opera usually casts its "supers," from an existing pool of talent, but occasionally they hold open auditions. So I signed up, and, it being a few blocks from Mike's school, I signed him up too.

A couple of weeks later, much to Mike's dismay, we got an email offering him a role as a Nibelung in *Das Rheingold*. So we made a deal. He would attend two rehearsals for the experience. If he didn't like it, he could quit. It actually only took one rehearsal and he was hooked.

As rehearsals were winding up, we received another email offering me a role as one of the Sbirri in *Tosca*. The email went on to say that they really enjoyed working with Mike, and the stage director for *Tosca* was adding stage business for five boys. They offered Mike one of the roles.

By the time rehearsals started for *Tosca*, Mike was an old hand. He knew the way around the rabbit warren of rooms and hallways under the Opera House, where all the costuming, make up, props, etc., are managed. He knew many of the stage hands and staff. I just followed him around, and it made him feel really grown up to know more than his dad.

Normally supers do not take curtain calls. But before the final dress rehearsal a notice was posted that because it was a new production, and we were "creating roles" for the first time, the supers would be given a curtain call on opening night.

So it was that as the final notes faded and the curtain fell, Mike and I filed out on the stage together. We took our positions, and moments later the curtain rose on 3,000 people applauding as we took our bows.

—Tim McCormick

# WILDERNESS LODGES AND READY-MADE CAMPING

**D**id you spend your childhood watching your father struggle and swear to back up a trailer into a narrow parking space, or try to remember how to set up the tent summer after summer? It is time to let him relax, and you can take over from here . . . but if setting up a tent or backing up a trailer isn't really your thing, there are now places that let you have the camping experience without the hassle of set up.

Airstream trailers are the hippest thing these days, and all around the country there are hotels that have turned the shiny aluminum trailers into comfy rooms you can rent. North of San Francisco in the heart of the Sonoma wine country is where you will find AutoCamp, where the trailers are outfitted like high end hotel rooms. Check them out at autocamp.com. Up in Oregon's Willamette Valley is where you will find The Vintages Trailer Resort, filled with restored retro trailers, the kind that fans called "canned hams" because of their distinct shape. On the outskirts of Ashville, North Carolina, you can stay at the JuneBug Retro Resort, in their collection of restored 50s and 60s campers and trailers.

Wilderness lodges are also a way to go if you and your dad are in pretty good shape and willing to hike to get there. In Massachusetts, Mount Greylock has the Bascom Lodge for about $40 per bunk. In California, the High Sierra Camp is far more comfortable but also quite a bit more expensive; it falls into the category of "glamping."

Even if your dad's trailer driving days are behind him, you can still get him out there in a folding chair to watch you struggle to light the campfire. Now it's his turn to laugh at your efforts.

"The one time I backed up a trailer, I snapped the safety chain," says Gin Sander. Staying in one of the emerging vacation spots that have trailers already in place means you won't need to know how to do this, but in case you do, rest assured that there are countless YouTube videos that promise to teach you how. Maybe you and your dad can watch one together for a laugh.

# BE A ROAD SCHOLAR

**W**hat was founded in 1975 as Elder Hostel has long since morphed into thousands of guided trips for those who are 55 and over. The trips are organized around various interests—jazz, barbecue, art history, architecture; no doubt there will be one that will align with your father's interests. And if you are older than 55 yourself, why not pack your bag and go along too?

Has your dad always wanted to go to spring training for his favorite baseball team? Road Scholar has a trip for that. Want to eat famous Kansas City BBQ and take in some local jazz? Road Scholar has a trip for that. These are not luxury trips though; the point is to keep the price within the range of affordability. Check out their offerings at roadscholar.org.

Since beginning in 2002, philanthropist Bernard Osher has funded well over a hundred Lifelong Learning Institutes at colleges and universities around the country, and new programs continue to open. For an annual membership fee of $20, members can enroll for free in Osher courses on topics like "The Constitution and American Values," "The Bible as Literature," "Best American Short Stories of the Twentieth Century," or "Codes, Codebreakers, and History." Check with the university nearest you to see if they have an Osher program.

# BRUSH UP YOUR SPANISH

**B**rush up your Spanish, French, Italian, Greek, or whatever language you and your father might want to work on together. Perhaps there is family history written in another language that you two can undertake to translate or he remembers a few words from childhood and would enjoy adding to his vocabulary and reminiscing about long past family members who spoke the languages.

Used bookstores and thrift stores are awash in old CDs, perhaps you can find a language program to listen together on a long car trip. You can also search out language podcasts. Anything that involves learning something new will not only help keep your father's mind sharp but will benefit you in the long run too! Multicultural food festivals are not to be missed, of course; the cuisine of whatever language you two are trying to improve your skills in will no doubt be delicious!

"Being a great father is like shaving. No matter how good you shaved today, you have to do it again tomorrow."

−Reed Markham

# SHARING ECONOMY

**W**ho isn't getting in on the sharing economy? Pretty much everyone is participating in some way, but maybe not yet your dad. There are specialty sites that help seniors get in the game, like silvernest.com, a homesharing platform for seniors. Unlike the vacation rental sites, this is focused on helping seniors find roommates to share housing costs. According to the World Economic Forum, future growth in the sharing economy will be driven by several groups, including the elderly.

Maybe he isn't ready to share his house or borrow someone else's. Here is a simpler way—if it's time for your dad to downsize, he can participate in the sharing economy by donating tools to the local library. Many libraries across the country are developing a department called the Library of Things that loans out equipment like sewing machines, word working tools, musical instruments, board games, all manner of things your father might be ready to part with so that someone else can enjoy them.

# FANTASY SPORTS CAMP

**D**oes your father get a nostalgic look in his eyes as he watches sports on TV? Perhaps it brings back memories of his younger days out on the field or the court. If he still has a dream of playing again, it might be time for him to go to camp. A fantasy camp, that is, like the one that Cal Ripkin runs in Myrtle Beach, Florida. These don't come cheap, of course, but it just might be the very kind of vacation your father has been dreaming of. Details are at ripkincamps.com, and you can also check out the camps that are run by the Minnesota Twins and the Atlanta Braves.

Is football his thing? Maybe he'd enjoy the fantasy camp that the Notre Dame football program runs. NDfootballfantasycamp.com has details. Basketball fanatics can drop the really big dough for the chance to hang out and play with Michael Jordan at his fantasy basketball camp, "Flight School." Details at MJflightschool.com.

Golfers? Yes, there is a fantasy camp for him that lets him experience what the pros do on tour. Pgatourexperience.com. And lastly, Dad can get out on the ice with Wayne Gretzky in Glendale, Arizona. Details at gretzky.com.

Too pricey? Well, why not just head out to the batting cage for the afternoon or dig out an old football to toss around on the lawn? Pick up two mitts at a garage sale and get out there to the park. It doesn't have to cost money for your dad to play a little sports with you.

# SHARING A SUNRISE

**W**atching the sunrise holds a personal meaning for each of us. The quiet and stillness of a new morning watching with amazement all the glory as a new day uniquely encourages us.. It is even better shared or better yet, shared with Dad. Have you considered rising at dawn with a thermos brimming with hot coffee, and Dad? How special it would be, magical even, to take Dad for coffee as the sun comes up. Get out the thermos and real coffee cups. You just might have a handed down red plaid travel thermos stored somewhere in the garage. Take the blankets and chairs. When have the two of you ever done this? If Dad is retired and likes to avoid crowds, arrange your work schedule to make it happen. There are opportunities for enjoying a sunrise every day.

You know the song from the *Fiddler on the Roof* musical—"Sunrise, Sunset"—so sad and mournful as Tevye reflects on how quickly his little girl has grown into womanhood. Watching a sunrise together might open your father up to sharing memories from your childhood that he remembers fondly.

# Unforgettable Father Moments

When we were growing up, there was this running joke in our family that grown-ups never make mistakes. I don't know exactly how it started. There was definitely an incident with a pancake, which my dad was trying to flip in the pan without using a spatula. Rather than admit that it had landed on his shoe as the result of bad planning (the spatula was likely in a nearby drawer), he insisted that this had happened because he'd noticed that his shoes needed a polish, and he'd wanted to test the cleaning properties of half-cooked pancakes. Because it certainly hadn't been a mistake. Grown-ups don't make those.

This family chestnut allowed us to giggle at the absurdity of whatever had gone wrong, and also to acknowledge that of course grown-ups were human too. As smart as he was (and is), my dad regularly reminded us that he didn't know everything. He was a single parent, and often sought out books and expert advice when he felt that he was in over his head raising three girls. Once, my sisters and I had been asking him (begging, really) to allow us to wear makeup. I presume he took one look at our artless application of whatever gaudy drugstore colors had appealed to us at the moment— but rather than point out how ridiculous it looked and tell us to wait a few years, he invited a Mary Kay lady to come to the house and teach us how to apply an appropriate amount of the right colors (and a thing or two about adolescent skin care).

Another time, prompted by what I assume was his final straw in listening to us squabble, he bought us each copies of *Getting to Yes*—a book on negotiation strategies written by two Harvard Business School professors. He figured, if it wouldn't help us stop fighting altogether, at least it would help us argue our points more effectively. I was ten.

Then there was the time, after the passing of my great-grandmother, that I asked him what happens when we die. The details of the discussion that followed are hazy, but I clearly remember him sharing several different philosophies, and telling me that this was a point on which many reasonable people disagree, and no one really knew for sure. This blew my mind. Both that there were so many beliefs, and that this big important thing was unknowable even to grown-ups. Even to my dad.

I think about these moments, so much more poignant now that I'm a parent myself. I see how much harder it is at any given moment to engage with the myriad of daily questions to which you have no easy answers than to simply shut them down. To say, "Look, kid—I'm as confused as you are about this one. Why don't we try to figure it out together?" Of course, now I'm the grown-up, so I get the privilege of claiming that I'm just polishing my shoe.

—Margaret Teichert

"A father's a treasure; a brother's a comfort; a friend is both."

–Benjamin Franklin

# SUNDAY SPECIAL

**N**ot all religions meet on Sunday, of course, but perhaps attending a service was a part of your family ritual when you were a kid. As an adult though, maybe your own attendance has sorta dropped off as the years have gone by. Does your father still go, though? Parents are always secretly pleased when their grown children come along to religious services with them. So even if you aren't the church-going type, it would be a very special gesture to accompany your father to his religious service a few times a year.

Attending religious services can play an important part in the lives of seniors, from fulfilling their spiritual needs to fulfilling their social needs. It can also help keep you healthy. A recent study by Vanderbilt University found that middle-aged adults who attended religious services at least once in the past year were half as likely to die prematurely as those who didn't.

The desire to come together with others is a basic human need, but not everyone wants to embrace organized religion. You might want to look into the Sunday Assembly movement for either yourself or your father. Founded in London in 2013 and now found in many locations in the US, Sunday Assembly is a non-religious gathering for folks who want to experience a communal feeling without religious overtones.

# TALL SHIPS

Relive those pirate stories and old black and white Errol Flynn movies by touring a tall wooden ship with your father. Tall ships abound across the globe, even in these days of power yachts, and you can find out where one will be docking near you by visiting the events page at tall-shipsnetwork,com. There are tall ship festivals, regattas, and parades that take place across North America and all over Europe as well.

Touring a tall wooden sailing ship gives a sense of awe at the craftsmanship that was required to build it, the seamanship that was required to sail it across uncharted waters, and the bravery that was required to step aboard and set sail for the horizon. Serious sailors can find opportunities to sign on as crew on some of these ships, and for serious cash you might be able to charter one.

# PIE DAY

**W**ho doesn't love pie? Freshly baked out of the oven, or a frothy whipped cream pie concoction? Pie has many fans—maybe you and your dad are among them. If so, scoop up your father some afternoon and go for a pie run. Is there a famed pie palace in your town? Many areas have them, from Sweet Delights in Miami, Florida (they specialize in key lime pie), to the Pie Snob in Phoenix, Arizona, and up to the Calico Cupboard in La Conner, Washington. You could plan an entire vacation around hunting for good pie if you were so inclined. In which case you'd both better bring along an extra, slightly larger, set of clothes.

National Pie Day is January 23rd (not to be confused with National Pi Day, on March 14th), so that might be a great time to plan your pie seeking adventures. If you can't wait that long, then how about tomorrow? A slice of pie is good anytime!

Where do these "National" days come from, anyway? They often start with folks just like you declaring a day to honor something they love. A nuclear engineer from Colorado, Charlie Papazian, was the first to declare his own birthday as National Pie Day and it was soon taken up and promoted by the American Pie Council.

# Unforgettable Father Moments

The treasure box was left for me when my dad passed away. It wasn't like the treasure box from the dentist's office or your favorite breakfast spot. It was, though, the treasures that Dad left for me to find after he was gone. I wouldn't have known about the True Detective stories written about several old cold case crimes he solved until I read them from the magazines stored in that old treasure box. I wouldn't have seen the medals honoring his military service or his valued career as a detective. I wouldn't have known this side of my dad.

Dad didn't brag or share those stories, but I did know him as an honorable man. He gave many valuable things to me, like teaching me to be independent and strong. He taught me to work hard with care and concern for others. These are some of my favorite things, but the best one happened each year on my birthday. He would call me and say, "I remember the day when we first met." His voice was kind, gentle, strong, and filled with love. Though we lived miles away, we were never closer.

—Jenyne Weingart

"A man's success is measured by what his wife and children say about him. Money and accomplishments mean nothing if you let your home fail."

—Tony Gaskins

# BACKYARD MOVIE NIGHT

**O**f course your father has a big screen television in his house and the ability to watch a favorite old film whenever he wants on the Turner Classic Movies channel. But wouldn't it be more fun and festive to set up a screen in the backyard, gather some family friends, pop up some popcorn, and pour your favorite candy into a bowl and host an outdoor movie night for your dad? Maybe you can show the very movie that your parents went to on their first date!

There might still be a pull up screen in your father's house left over from the days of watching slide shows, or you can certainly find one at a thrift store. For outdoor movies you can improvise by hanging a sheet, show the movie against a wall, or spring for one of the blow-up screens that are available from online retailers.

# BECOME A SCRIBE

The art of letter writing has faded in our tech-focused world, but few things are as much of a treat as a hand-written missive. Perhaps your father has been meaning to reach out to an old friend but needs a hand to make it happen. From buying the paper or greeting cards to helping him compose exactly what he wants to convey and then popping it in the mail, you can make this happen. It could become a regular ritual that you two can share, sitting down and writing out a letter or card to a new person each time.

> And none will hear the postman's knock
>
> Without a quickening of the heart
>
> For who can bear to feel himself forgotten?
>
> —W. H. Auden

# WALK ON

**H**eading out the door for a long walk is good for us all, and when combined with the do-gooder aspect of a charity walk, we can feel twice as good. What is your father's favorite cause? Perhaps there is an organized fund-raising walk that will fit the bill. In the spring and the fall, in every community across the land, there are 5k and 10k runs and walks that you can participate in. Walking together for a few miles in the midst of a crowd of people all donating their time and money to the same end is a great way to connect with both your family and your community.

Ordinary as it sounds, walking is good for us. If a 5k walk is too far at this point in your father's life, then maybe just a stroll around the block is in order. However long you walk, wherever it takes you, will benefit you both. Just walking for 21 minutes a day, for 2.5 hours a week, can cut heart disease by 30 percent. It is also a mood booster, so helps lift the spirits for anyone who is feeling low. So open the door and usher your father outside. You'll be glad you did.

"It is a wise father that knows his own child."

–William Shakespeare

# STAND UP AND SPEAK

The Toastmasters International organization has been around for decades, and for decades, members have been coming weekly to improve their public speaking skills. The ability to stand in front of an audience and deliver can be a major boost not only to career advancement but also for increased self-confidence and improved social skills. Sound like something you and your father could benefit from? Why not find a chapter near you and join together? The very first required speech in the Toastmasters program is called the Icebreaker, where new members deliver a three-minute talk about themselves. Who knows what you might learn about yourself and your family by listening to your father's Icebreaker?

Even if your father is past the active career stage of life, Toastmasters Clubs are filled with interesting people holding interesting weekly meetings. You might hear an inspirational speech, an informational speech, and a humorous speech, all while you are eating your lunch or breakfast (clubs meet at all different times, there will always be one that works with your schedule). Find a group near you at toastmasters.org.

# HONOR FLIGHTS

**D**id your father serve in the military? If so, he may well qualify for one of the Honor Flights that leave from all over the country and head to our nation's capital. Founded in 2005, the Honor Flight Network has so far taken more than 200,000 vets to Washington, DC, to visit the National World War II Memorial.

Originally focused on vets of WWII, they are now also honoring those who served in the Korean and Vietnam Wars with flights to Washington, DC. Wayne Heple, a veteran of the Korean War, recently took part in a flight along with his son Larry, who'd come along as a companion. Due to the age of the participants, bringing along a friend or family member is a requirement. "Overall, the hospitality everywhere we went was exceptional," Wayne said. "And so tightly organized; it was like watching a world class symphony perform a masterpiece."

You can find out more information about the organization and their trips at Honorflight.org.

> Each December there is a touching tribute to our fallen soldiers called Wreathes Across America. You can sign up to volunteer at wreathsacrossamerica.org.

# Unforgettable Father Moments

I see my dad in front of me, the hospital bed envelops his body, crisp white linens tucked up to his chest, his arms out to his sides, resting on the sheets, palms up. Eyes closed, his mouth shaping an unnatural "O" around the tube pushing air into his lungs. The quietness of the room, the stillness, allowed me entrance, gave way to my steps as I approached Dad. I extend my left hand and place it under his right hand, folding my fingers over his, pressing gently. I scoot closer. Leaning in, I cup the side of Dad's face with my left hand and pat back the soft grays of his temples with my right, and kiss him softly on his forehead, and once more.

"I love you, Dad," I hear myself say. And it doesn't sound strange, this whispered confession. This is no secret, I'm thinking, still caressing Dad's face, smiling this time and saying, "Dad, it's me, your number three!" and I hear some laughter from the other family members in the room. It doesn't wake or rouse him, though. Dad doesn't suddenly sense my presence and squeeze my hand, nor does he open his eyes. I sit down next to Aunt Kathy, and we find ourselves staring into Dad's face as if it has all the answers we've ever needed.

The priest comes and says his blessings, asks us to pray for Rosendo "Roy" Mauricio, and help him find his way home. Home, he says. The attending physician enters the room, adjusts the morphine drip, nods to me, "It won't be long." We all inch closer to the bed. Speechless. Stunned. It's 4:50 p.m. on Sunday, December 19, 2010, and Dad is gone.

At the foot of his bed, I can't stop looking at his face, the same face that I see, that I saw at his kitchen table on West Lafayette, decades ago, playing poker with his brothers, beckoning everyone to place their bets and "Get this show on the road." Dad sees me enter the kitchen through the rounded doorway, suddenly stands and throws out his arms in mock surprise and shouts, "Ruby-Duby-Doo!" (his silly nickname for me) and says, "I love you, kiddo!"—And I remember how my face felt then, how I could feel that smile, his smile becoming mine. Dad hugs me and I feel his strong arms encompassing me, holding me. I have his full Mauricio-lips, his warm brown eyes, his heartbreaking hugs. And it's those heartbreaking hugs that will stay with me always. Always.

—Rueben Mauricio

# THE NOTE

**W**rite a handwritten note to your dad. It could be silly or serious but most of all, it must be sincere. Remind him of something that he's done that sticks in your mind. He may have forgotten or maybe he never knew how important it was to you. Write about just one thing. A father doesn't always have the experience of seeing your handwriting, especially in today's world. It promises to add value to his memories of you.

Writing a letter is probably easier than listing all the reasons of why your father is a great father. It doesn't need to be a long letter. What is written in a note will become a lasting memory. Do you remember opening a handwritten letter from your dad? Do you recall holding it for a while before reading it because you've never received a letter from him before? It promises to be a personal experience for you. It works the other way around too. And, you can do it anytime for any reason.

A loved one's handwriting is a popular tattoo. There is a name for it: "Memory tattoos." Finding an unexpected note written in your father's handwriting can be both jolting and endearing.

"Dads are most ordinary men turned by love into heroes, adventurers, storytellers, and singers of song."

—Unknown

# CLOSE SHAVE

When was the last time you went for a haircut with your dad? Maybe it's time to share a haircut together. Has your dad always gone to the same barber? If so, listen in to the banter—their relationship continues in conversation every four or five weeks; you will likely be intrigued with their interaction. Take a selfie with your dad or a photo of your dad and his barber, then turn it into a Father's Day card. You'll learn something new about your dad as you share a meaningful and lasting experience that includes a trim.

Barbers are suddenly hip these days, and what was considered an old-fashioned job is now highly sought after by a new crop of young men entering the profession. So maybe you should take your dad to your barber instead and let him see how the barbershop world is changing.

> Barbering is an ancient and honorable profession originating in the middle ages that included surgical procedures like pulling teeth and bloodletting.

# GEAR UP WITH DAD

**D**ad has taught us pretty good stuff about behavior, manners, and household responsibilities. If you were lucky, he taught you some basic skills: how to use a slide ruler, change the oil in your car, mow the lawn, and perhaps even fix the fence. But now, he would probably get a kick out of you asking him to teach you something new like a sport, fishing, or using a gun or a bow and arrow. Gear up with Dad. He probably has some things you can dig out of him and out of an old storage shed and, in the process, you will discover one of his old passions.

Can you think of an old photo of your father wearing gear? Where is it? What became of it? Is it framed somewhere around his house? Imagine a photo with you and your Dad wearing high waders and geared up for fly fishing. It is never too late to learn something new together. We can imagine the laughter, the awkwardness, and the joy of catching a trout and cooking it, together. A shared experience like this can end up being the beginning of a family tradition, an unforgettable memory.

# Unforgettable Father Moments

Uncle Elmer's barber shop was located across the street from the courthouse in my old town. It only had one barber chair, which was usually occupied. I would stop in and visit when passing through. If he was cutting hair, I would sit and wait in one of four other chairs that lined the wall and we would talk between customers. Sometimes he'd share a story that I hadn't heard before. Sometimes the stories were familiar. Sometimes they included stories about his brother, my dad.

On this day he was sitting in the barber chair waiting for his next appointment. He said he wanted to work until his nine-tieth birthday next year. Then he would retire. He told me about a young man with two kids that came by for a haircut. When Elmer was done cutting his hair the man looked at his watch and said, "Could I leave my kids here for just a little while? I have a court date. Can you trim up their hair, and I'll be back as soon as I can?"

Puzzled, I asked, "What did you do?"

"Ah heck, I cut both kids' hair. He still didn't come back. I started wondering what was going on and I was getting hungry, you know? But the kids were good; they just sat there fidgeting, looking around. So, I gave them each a half

of my sandwich, cut up the apple, and gave them a glass of water. What else could I do? I was just hoping that the guy wasn't going to jail for something. I didn't know. But those kids didn't need to worry. That guy walked out without paying for his haircut, left his kids with me, and I didn't know if I'd see him before I closed up shop," he went on.

As I thought about all of this, I couldn't imagine leaving my kids with a stranger. Then I realized the guy didn't think of himself as a stranger.

"Yeah, he finally came back, dropped a $50 bill on the counter, said 'let's go' to the kids, and left. Can you imagine that?" he added.

—Cathy MacHold

# VISIT A NATIONAL PARK

**W**ith our busy day-to-day lives, obligations, planned vacations, and holidays, how much quality time have you actually shared one-on-one with your father? Twenty-nine states have accessible national parks. Visiting national parks is quite a popular bucket list item! We think sharing the adventure with Dad should be bumped up to the top of the list. In the US, we have the ability to enjoy 61 protected lands, each unique, special, and amazing like nothing else in our world. Within the parks we can fish, swim, explore, hike, view historical objects, unique geological features, and ecosystems. We can enjoy great animal experiences like finding an elk herd, moose in the wild, bison herds, or find rare birds, like albatross. Imagine seeing wildlife that can't be found anywhere else on earth and sharing the experience with Dad. You may remember being a child seated in the backseat of the family car as you read the national park signs that you passed on the way to somewhere else. Well, now is the time to share that curiosity with Dad. He just might surprise you with his ideas of which park to explore first.

Who doesn't want to stay in a national park and never leave? Well, then why not volunteer and get the chance to stay on? There are opportunities in almost every national park; check out the listings at volunteer.gov to see what is available at your favorite destination.

"Never go on trips with anyone you do not love."

–Ernest Hemingway

# THE OLYMPIC PARK EXPERIENCE

**W**hen you hear the term "Olympic Park," you might visualize a once-great place that hosted the Olympics. Your thoughts might then take you to, *How long ago was that?* But, think again. Part of the legacy for the selected host city is the benefit of what remains. These unique and special venues offer inviting activities such as an aquatics complex, cycling tracks, Nordic skiing, hockey rinks, and more. Sites like Squaw Valley USA was laid out so that most of the venues are within walking distance. Have you ever seen the height of an Olympic-size ski jump? Squaw Valley is open all year. The downtown Los Angeles Sports Park includes Exposition Park, which was used during the 1932 and 1984 games. Things to do at the Utah Olympic Park include adventures such as zip lining, bobsledding, and free-style acrobatic feats. You can join in or watch, whichever Dad wants.

Michael Adams was an eight-year-old along for the ride, lugging gear for his father when late one afternoon his dad pulled the old station wagon to the side of a country road and jumped out. "I remember the rush, rush, rush," Adams told an interviewer. The result was "Moonrise, Hernandez, New Mexico," one of Ansel Adams's most famous black and white images.

# SNOW DAY

Even if neither of you ski, you can enjoy the experience and beauty of a winter's day and the drive to the mountains together. Bundle up in your warmest clothing—don't forget your mittens, hat, and non-slippery shoes. Find a resort trail map so you can follow the skiers and make sense of where they are coming from. Find a restaurant or bar with a fireplace and large window where you can watch the skiers, the families, and all the goings-on. Order a hot cocoa or a hot toddy of your liking. Enjoy resort food, chili, or a French hotdog with mustard.

Skiing is an all-time-favorite thing to do for many, but not-so-much for others. As good sports, willing non-skiers can go and watch. There are ski resorts where moms wear fur coats and the signs are triplicated in English, Japanese, and Italian. The world opens up when you explore the passions of others. If you can and it's available, learn to drive or ride a piste basher. You might recognize the name as a snow grooming caterpillar.

# Unforgettable Father Moments

My younger sister Sandra and I didn't see our dad much when we were growing up. He worked swing-shift so he would be sleeping when we left for school and was gone to work when we got home from school. On the weekends he was mostly busy with things that needed to be done around the house or working on the car. I don't have many memories of doing things with my dad in those early years, but I do remember that if I asked a question about something I didn't understand, he would try to take the time to explain it to me.

One of those weekend days when he was in the driveway working on his car, it occurred to me that if I showed interest in what he was doing it could lead to some time with him. I went outside and asked him if he could explain to me how an engine works—not such a simple, easily answered question when there is work that needs to be done. Not only did he go through the entire engine explaining how it worked, he wrote down on paper how the less visible parts of the car worked with the engine. I didn't quite understand everything then, but I still have those drawings 30+ years later.

—Sharon Goodwin

# INTO THIN AIR

Years ago, there was an article in *Parade* magazine, once included with the Sunday newspaper, asking, "What Type of Vacation Would Bill Gates Take?" The idea still sticks in our minds because at the time it seemed out of reach. In today's world, it is very possible. Perhaps you've heard of Heli-Skiing? Well, the same company created Heli-Hiking and that is what Bill Gates did on a particular vacation. One offered experience is called Lodge to Lodge. A helicopter picks you up at a remote area where you are taken by bus. If you don't all fit into the twelve seats, the helicopter comes back and makes another trip. You are delivered to the first lodge, trained and fitted with equipment, then off you go for your first day of a week of serious hiking. The helicopter drops you at the base in any of the many places in the Canadian mountain Rockies. You hike all day with trained and experienced mountaineers, a packed lunch is included, then the helicopter returns you. If you consider the great outdoors, the challenges, the animal encounters, and the best conversations with Dad, it is by far an all-time great adventure.

Bill Gates also suggests vacationing in Australia. While waiting in line for a Sydney Bridge Climb, you will see a Bill Gates photo in the overhead slide-show of guests who have enjoyed the bridge climb adventure. Imagine the thrill of experiencing two of Bill Gates's vacation choices.

# Unforgettable Father Moments

There were only thirty seconds left in the final game of the season. The home team was ahead, but from the two-yard line they were going for one more touchdown. Number 52, a senior in his last game, usually played defense. Yet there he was, formed up beside the quarterback.

Then came the snap, the hand off to #52, and the entire team formed up around him driving him forward toward the goal line. The ref's whistle screamed; hands went up. "Touchdown!" The secret play they had been practicing for weeks had paid off, and #52 was carried off the field on his team's shoulders.

My wife and I first met #52 in a neonatal ICU. His birth-mother was a high school senior who had hidden the pregnancy and received no prenatal care. She went into labor post-term, and barely got to the hospital in time for an emergency c-section. The birth family wanted to have the baby adopted. A mutual friend put them in touch with my wife's aunt, who knew we were considering adoption. She called us and we flew to Portland to meet the girl and her family. We all agreed we should adopt #52.

Later we met with the doctors and found out that #52 had no vital signs at birth except a pulse and was barely saved.

We also found out that he was born with methamphetamine in his system. We asked what this all meant. They told us he appeared fine now, and so was unlikely to be severely affected, but also it was all but certain he would have some long-term effects.

Then we parked ourselves in a Starbucks, and talked for hours. In the end, the chance to offer him the resources of the San Francisco area, should he need them, and the risks of our alternatives prevailed. Weeks later, with the stroke of a judge's pen, I became #52's dad.

It took almost a year before we noticed #52 wasn't developing normally. Several doctor visits later we received the diagnosis: #52 has cerebral palsy. Years of intensive occupational and physical therapy began, and there were doubts his physical functioning would ever be near normal.

But he was having none of that. He overcame every obstacle and mainstreamed all through school. We called him "the work around kid." So it was no big surprise when he announced he had asked to work out with his friends on the football team, or when he asked the coach to try out for JV and made the team, and then varsity a year later.

The touchdown? That was a surprise.

But that's just who he is, and I get to be his dad every day.

—Tim McCormick

# SHARE A DREAM

**S**hare a dream of yours with your dad. It could be old or new, recent or one to come. Then spend time dreaming together. Perhaps start with "Let's spend our Lottery Winnings." Dream that you won 300 million tax-free dollars. How would you spend them? It's an infectious thought. Encourage Dad to join in. Sometimes our generations separate us, but this one could prove to be enlightening.

You can also try sharing your actual dreams, the movies that run in your head every night while sleeping. Start the conversation by sharing what your wild dream was last evening, and ask your father what he dreamt. "Nothing," might be the answer, or "I don't remember." Well, then ask about a dream he does remember.

If you can get your father talking about what he dreams at night, perhaps you can get him to write them down. A blank journal is always a nice gift—encourage him to fill the pages with his nightly movies.

"A father is neither an anchor to hold us back, nor a sail to take us there, but a guiding light whose love shows us the way."

—Unknown

# FAMOUS BIRTHDAY PARTY CELEBRATIONS

"**M**y father's birthday is the same as Albert Einstein's," one friend told us. "So every year instead of throwing a party, baking a cake, or buying a card for my own father, we do it for Einstein. And then, oh yeah, maybe also this other guy too, the one who is actually sitting there with us at the table. He loves it because that way not only does it take on a joking tone but also allows him to deflect the usual birthday attention. He doesn't like to be in the spotlight, so this way he is sort of standing next to the spotlight, slightly off stage."

Does your father have the same birthday as a famous person? Find out at famousbirthdays.com and start planning that party!

# KEYS TO THE FERRARI . . .

Has your father always secretly (or not-so-secretly) longed to drive a high-end performance car like a Maserati, a Ferrari, or a James Bond-like Aston Martin? Or perhaps swan around town in a toney Bentley in the manner of to the manor born? It is possible to give him the experience for a short time, anyway. Many of the well-known car rental agencies have high end departments that rent specialty cars.

Hertz has a Prestige Collection that rents Mercedes and Range Rovers, and Enterprise has a division called Exotic Cars Collection that rents Aston Martins, Bentleys, Ferraris, Maseratis, and Lamborghinis.

If renting a fast car for an afternoon isn't in the budget, take a look at the picture book 100 Dream Cars that A. J. Baime, the weekly car columnist for the Wall Street Journal, has put together from his favorite columns. It is filled with photos and the stories of how the cars were acquired. Maybe your dad has a story about his car that you should write down?

# *Unforgettable Father Moments*

On any given day, you can now find fathers walking the park or cruising the coffee shop with little babies strapped to their chest. That's really a new thing. Certainly, there have always been fathers who loved their children and were involved in their lives in many ways. But since women have become way more involved in the work force in the past few decades, fathers have had the opportunity to begin quietly breaking into a new world. The realm of newborn, infant, baby care with all its challenges and joys is finally an opportunity allowed to, and welcomed by, men. And many men are now stepping into this role that was largely denied to their fathers and grandfathers.

Think about it, moms. If you felt clueless when your babies were born, just imagine the terror of a man who's never had the skills of early fatherhood modeled for him. And baby care has, in all probability, not exactly been on his radar as he has grown into adulthood. It might be easier for him to stand back, pleading incompetency, or run away. Yet, many men find they want the chance to care for their newborn. They want the experience and connection that comes from changing the diapers, and feeding bottles of milk, and rocking to sleep, and meeting the many needs of their children.

My husband has said that he wouldn't trade that time for anything. The sleepless nights, despite the poop explosions, the inconsolable infants, the feverish babies, the vomiting and spitting up, despite all the exhausting physical and emotional challenges of those first years, he wouldn't trade them for a more distant relationship. He treasures the intimacy of all that time loving and caring for and raising his kids. He is also immensely proud of his hard-won, hard-learned skills in juggling two babies at the same time!

There is a continuous revolution going on in fatherhood, and it is a tremendous opportunity for men. Because every day is a father's day.

—Kathleen Cawley

# GRAVEYARD VISITS

Sounds pretty gloomy, an afternoon at the cemetery. But it doesn't have to be—instead it can be a way to learn more about your family if your father has stories to share about the family members buried there. And it can be a way to feel closer to those who have gone before us. "I was leading a weekend history tour through a local graveyard and noticed a man and his wife at a large family plot," literary historian Julia Berenson told us. "As it was one of the historic families that I was talking about anyway we soon struck up a conversation. 'I came to have a beer with my dad,' the man said, 'It's Father's Day and I do this every year.' He pulled out a six pack of beer, popped two of them open, poured one on his father's grave, and then drank one himself."

"Patience is the biggest thing my father taught me in the kitchen. When I was growing up, he would make an amazing rum and raisin eggless ice cream that required long hours of stirring, and then it had to freeze overnight. He showed me that it takes time to create deliciousness."

—Maneet Chauhan

# VISIT A VETERAN'S CEMETERY ON VETERANS DAY

Even if your dad didn't serve, he can still honor those that have, and we all know someone. Visiting a National Cemetery is humbling. You can enjoy the ceremony, the military songs, the service members in attendance. It is a time-honored reminder of the dedication of all branches of our military. Maybe your father would enjoy visiting a gravesite of a loved one or, perhaps, of an old buddy.

Remember that there is a difference in the two holidays that honor vets—Veterans Day is designated as a day to honor all veterans of the Armed Forces, and Memorial Day is designated as the day to honor those who have fallen while fighting for the country.

Build a shadowbox with him using the buttons and medals from his old uniform. Ask him questions. Why did you receive this one or that one? Ask if he wants to share any of his experiences. Since you've likely not seen him in his uniform, maybe he will model it for you. Those who have served should be honored. The time they served should be valued and remembered that because they served, we, fortunately, did not have to.

# GIVE A COMPLIMENT

**Y**es, this sounds like such a simple thing to do, but be prepared as this could bring you to tears. Be sincere, look him in the eye, face to face. Make him see that you mean it. Then, ask your father if he wants to give you a compliment. Remember, you had the time to think about it and prepare. You might want to give him time to think about it too.

If your parents are still an item, do you know where your mother's wedding dress is? Possibly stored in a closet as so many beloved dresses are. Can you get it out and show Dad? Without a word, wait for his reaction. Ask him to tell you about "his" wedding day. Ask him to share the most romantic thing he did and why it was important. It could be that he remembers something entirely different than your mother does.

# Unforgettable Father Moments

It's not the old worn shorts or the T-shirt that a washing might ruin. It's not the economy car with the holes cut into the sides that he called screen doors or the disregard for the funny reactions of the drivers passing him by. It's not how easily my new father-in-law Mac added himself to our lives with love and generosity, but it was how much of him became a big part of our day-to-day lives. We didn't know how much we missed him until he arrived.

His gruff and generous character with a sparkle in his eyes and a smirk on his face waited for us to return from work. He'd line up Ritz Crackers with peanut butter and jelly fixed on a platter, three for each for the three of us. He'd ask about our day then complain about the dog and the cat and why did we have to name Max, our Brittany Spaniel, that name?

He talked to the neighbors and told us what was going on in the neighborhood. He told us not to bother about his trailer parked out back by the shed. He could clean it himself. He mowed using the riding lawn mower and didn't know that was ground cover that he mowed over but said, "Don't worry, it'll come back better." And it did.

He'd show us the picture of his wife who was lost to cancer and tell us how much he missed her. She was pretty and he knew that we would like her. He was glad that she didn't have to suffer anymore, but he still missed her.

When it got too cold, he was going to the desert because he like to wear his shorts all year long. He would take his motorcycle or maybe his 28-year old Ford pickup truck. He wasn't sure. And he'd come back when the desert got cold and it was warmer here.

Then we'd enjoy dinner, and Mac would ask, "Why did you have to name that dog Max? I always think you're calling me."

—Claire Manon

# HELPING HANDS

**A**s we progress further along on our sentimental journey, have you considered asking your dad what he needs help with? He might surprise you. It's not uncommon for someone to hesitate about asking for help or asking for what they truly need. It's such an easy thing. Cathy MacHold's dad drove a cement truck, pretty heavy work at times. But later in life even he needed help with heavy things. "When he moved, he wanted his backyard walkway redone and mentioned it. When he said something like that in the past, it was done, pronto. But the next time I visited; the walkway was still undone. He didn't mention it but walked me around back. I didn't get the dropped hint. Then one day it hit me all at once. Of course he wanted a new walkway added to his yard. Because he wasn't able to do the work as he once could, he was unsure of what to do. He was beginning to use a wheelchair and it was the only way he could get around in his backyard."

# DAD'S FRIENDS

**W**ho are your father's friends? Do you know them all? If not, tell him you'd like to meet his friends. Is there one he'd like to visit? Accompany him. You could make this a road trip and explore interesting places along the way. Drive the roads that he shared with his friends. Both of you will benefit from unexpected treasures. If you have met Dad's friends previously but never truly got to know them, you might even arrange a surprise lunch. You might consider hosting a dinner party for Dad and a few of his friends; his job is to select the menu, maybe it should be something his mom cooked or something vintage—fancy or not, he'll appreciate the event with big smiles. Whatever direction you take from this will provide interesting insights about your father from a new perspective.

Jim Rohn, the entrepreneur, author, motivational speaker, and mentor to self-help god Tony Robbins, famously said, "You are the average of the five people you spend the most time with."

# ASK QUESTIONS AND MORE QUESTIONS

**W**hy are questions uncomfortable for some, especially older generations? Maybe it's because the questions are too deep or that the answers have not been previously said out loud. Maybe it's because they are personal or perhaps because when your father was growing up, he was to be seen and not heard, part of the Baby Boomer Generation. Don't wait to discover the answers. Tip toe into them. What was the saddest day of his life? The happiest? The most difficult? The most challenging? Did he enjoy his career? What would he have changed? What is his greatest fear? What does he still want to do in life?

Create a crossword puzzle adding information using his answers with alternative solutions or comments and mail it to him. The trick would be asking the questions, so your dad doesn't feel "drilled" or "interviewed." He will enjoy the fact that you actually "listened" and did something with his words.

The Story of "Dance with My Father"

The song by Luther Vandross is a real tearjerker. He wrote "Dance with My Father" with Richard Marx, based on his own personal experience. It is a tribute to his father, Luther Vandross, Sr., who died due to complications of diabetes when Luther was seven. Luther's most poignant memory of his dad was his dancing in the house with his kids, which is where the concept of the song came from.

"You are stuck with me till the world falls to pieces, and if we're not still standing even then we'll still find a way to be together."

–Ottilie Weber

# OPEN YOUR HEART

Opening your heart is not an easy task. Direct questions can be very uncomfortable, but the goal in doing so is not to judge but to understand with the benefit of growing closer. You might begin with a confession. Tell Dad something about your childhood that he never knew. Make a confession. It's possible that he will reciprocate. "Tell me a secret, Dad"—this may or may not work. But if it does, it could be very interesting. Then reciprocate.

Talk about your feelings and how you feel as a result of opening your heart. Websites are readily available through search engines for finding seminars, classes, and other personal relationship-building techniques. Keep it positive and with purpose.

Singer-songwriter John Mayer's song "Daughters" is a message to fathers to nurture their daughters in their childhood, as their connection will affect their future relationships with men as adults. He uses his own troubled lover as an example.

# COME TO THE TABLE

**W**ho doesn't love to eat? If you do the math, how many meals have you shared with your dad? Could be a pretty big number if you think back to the baby, child, teenage era at three-plus meals a day. Now ask yourself, is there one culinary experience that stands out the most? You might have great childhood memories of grilling steaks in the backyard, or perhaps that didn't happen often enough, but you can make it possible now. Create new memories starting now by choosing one of these ideas:

- Pull out your BBQ cookbook, select a recipe, and create a shared experience.

- If your morning passion is coffee, create your own coffee-tasting experience with Dad.

- What's Dad's favorite beverage? Take a walk in a vineyard and learn from each other. Find a brandy blending class or go whiskey and scotch tasting.

- Introduce Dad to a new food. Has he ever tried sushi or Thai? Show him how to use chop sticks with the invitation.

- What is Dad's favorite dessert? Do a tasting of different ones. Make it a big deal.

- What is Dad's favorite takeout? Surprise him often and set up the eating place outdoors or at the formal dining table set in a very special way.

- Hold your own cooking class. What does Dad want to learn to make? Pie, cookies? Learn together. Teach one another.

- Each of you select a food channel cooking show. Watch together.

- Share your dad's favorite appetizer with him, even if it's Ritz Crackers with peanut butter and jelly.

# Unforgettable Father Moments

"There is no right way. The experience of losing someone is different every time." Those consoling words came from a business associate in 1987 when I told him my father had died and I didn't know how I was supposed to react.

I had not experienced death before, not even the death of grandparents, because I didn't know either my maternal or paternal grandparents.

Mom, one of six girls, came to San Francisco after high school because there were no jobs for girls in the lead mines of Bonne Terre, Missouri. She never saw her parents again and rarely spoke of them.

My paternal grandfather emigrated from Sweden in 1912 to establish a home for his family in the new world, but my paternal grandmother was afraid to cross the ocean. In 1914 she sent my father (age sixteen) with his sister (age thirteen) on a ship from Stockholm to Ellis Island. The children never saw their mother again. It was as if she never existed.

Pop eventually made his way to San Francisco; my aunt and grandfather settled in Los Angeles. When grandfather died, I was so young that I don't remember his visits.

The one emotion I remember feeling when my dad died was that of disappointment. He had not left me a letter or anything personal that was just between us. I knew he gave me life but thought he did not love me because he didn't write me a final note.

In my sixties, I took up photography. At the opening reception of my first solo photography show, a guest remarked that my images captured a unique view of the world and asked me how I learned to see. No one had ever asked me that before. As I explained to her how my father trained me to see, it was an epiphany to realize that my father did love me. He had given me a gift that no one else could, he taught me to see through the eyes of an artist, from the smallest details and marriage of colors to the nuances of ever-changing light and shadow throughout the day.

In addition to his gift of teaching me to see, he gave me a tiny diamond ring, the only Swedish family heirloom that exists in my family. It was presented to me by my father, who said it was given to him by his mother to give to his daughter on her 16th birthday. Pop was sixty-six when I turned sixteen. He had carried that fragile ring for fifty years.

In those two efforts, I now recognize his gifts of devotion and I understand that love manifests itself in many different ways and can remain openly hidden, just waiting for the right time to be seen.

—Ingrid Lundquist

"One father is more than a hundred schoolmasters."

-George Herbert

# THE SIMPLEST THINGS

**S**ometimes it is just the simplest things, mainly paying attention and giving of time, which can bring the happiest and most appreciated memories with Dad. He will never forget these acts of kindness and selflessness from you.

"What bugs you about your house, Dad?" Ask him. He just might surprise you with his answers. Maybe he would benefit from some decluttering. Perhaps invest time with a few good donation boxes. Be prepared for the unexpected like a decorating complaint around the house. Maybe what he would enjoy most would be an update of new curtains, pillows, something that he's grown tired of. You can probably easily help him with this. It might seem silly and unmanly but, take dad to a fabric store and have him feel the fabrics. Once you slyly discover what his preference is, make something from the fabric that will add quality to his daily experience like pillowcases, throw pillows, a table runner, or maybe even potholders.

Find out what your dad's least favorite thing to do is, and help him with it. It might be interesting to find out why it's not favorable and what it requires to turn it around into something better.

# Unforgettable Father Moments

I don't know if it was because we are both Virgos or not, but my dad and I had a communication that went beyond us speaking words. We seemed to know what each other was thinking or wanted without actually talking. During October and November when it rained, we spent a lot of time together. He would pick me up from school and together we prepared dinner so that it was ready when Mom came home from work.

On one of these fall days, I got kicked out of school for fighting. I was so scared to tell Dad. I sat on the step in the garage waiting for him to arrive home from work. When I told him he asked me who started the fight? Who hit who first? I said that she hit me, so I grabbed her by the back of her hair and put my knee into her nose, and blood went everywhere. He started laughing, then said, "I wouldn't expect you to allow someone to hit you and you not fight back." He added, "You did what I would have expected you to do: fight back." I was relieved as we both laughed. He wanted to know how bad I hurt her. "Blood was everywhere, especially from her nose," I said, "but a teacher came and stopped us and sent us to the dean." As I think back, I now see that in 1970 attitudes were rapidly changing. It was okay for a girl to get into a fight and get kicked out of school. It was okay for me as a girl to stand up for myself.

—Cyndi Tidd

# BOTTOMS UP!

If a holiday or family gathering is approaching, you might suggest to Dad that you create a toast for the next family meal together, sharing why family members are important and why they are individually special. This could be the best-established tradition that will be carried on for years to come.

According to a 2017 Pew Research Center survey, 44 percent of men aged eighteen to forty-nine years old hope to become fathers at some point. Maybe you have an uncle or brother who isn't a father. Think outside the box. Share any of our ideas with him. He'll treasure you forever.

"(My father) has always provided me a safe place to land and a hard place from which to launch."

–Chelsea Clinton

# GOING ON THE RECORD

**M**usic prompts memories. Why not get your father talking about the music in his life and make a voice recording of what he has to say? Save it for the next generations using up-to-date technologies. Record an audio-visual of Dad and make a YouTube video together. If he needs a little tech training, use this opportunity. There is probably a great deal about your dad that you don't know. What is his favorite song and why is it his favorite? Does he play a musical instrument? When did he learn to play? Who is his favorite musical artist? Learn to play a song with him. Or, sing it with him. Or, if he enjoys musicals or plays, take him to a live performance. Make a date with Dad to go see a local high school play or something new coming to your area.

# Unforgettable Father Moments

Dad left for work first, and was home by the time Mom arrived home from her day at work. She would open the door and walk in. Their eyes would meet—they were like magnets. He would embrace her, and she embraced him back. Then, they shared one big lingering kiss. My sisters and I could feel the sparks. We giggled. We always waited to watch the kiss. The minute we heard her car, we would stop what we were doing because we didn't want to miss it.

There were other things too. Dad showed me how he kept three $100 bills hidden in the back of his wallet. He said he waited for a SALE sign at Mom's favorite dress shop. When he saw it, he had the money to buy her dresses for work and then surprise her. He worked out a system with the shop owner. He'd pick out several dresses that he thought Mom would like and bring them home for her to try on. If she didn't like them or if they didn't fit, he could return them. He'd show us the dresses lined up on their bed. We'd giggle more, all of us waiting for the sound of Mom's car. *Shhhhh*, he'd hush us. We silently watched that kiss.

It was like that all through our time at home. The sparks were there as long as I can remember. They were true and loyal. They showed us how love could be. They showed us how to show love. As we grew in our lives, we discovered how special and rare it was to have parents with that kind of a special bond. We were lucky to see the sparks.

—Cathy MacHold

# THE OLD COUNTRY

**E**stablishing family traditions leads into family heritage. Ask Dad about your family heritage. Do a DNA test together and wait for the results. Research family history for an amazing journey together. Share an ancestry project with Dad. Gather the family history through scrapbooks or files that Dad has and move forward with an ancestry website. This project might take a while. It could start with a community information class and continue with online information. Most ancestry-type websites that are available include an enormous database. It requires a commitment of time to check and recheck information so that your family history is verifiable. This is a great project when you have a committed allowance of time available. Be prepared to discover more about your family history than you believed possible. This is also an opportunity to collect old family photos, identify family members, and organize the information including letters, cards, and other important historical data that Dad has collected over his life.

# CONTRIBUTORS

**Matías Bombal** is a man of extraordinary talents in the entertainment field—a professional master of ceremonies, a movie reviewer and radio personality, a documentarian, and an expert in the music of the 1920s and 30s, as well as classic films. You can find more about him at mabhollywood.com.

**Kathleen Cawley** is a physician's assistant, a writer, and mom to nine-year-old twins. Late in life, she married an industrious man who told stories of a wild and crazy youth. Assured of his new-found maturity, Kathleen agreed to start a family with this man whose smile grew wider when she argued with him and who could match her pun for pun. Kathleen offers help navigating modern parenthood in her book blog at shockofparenthood.com.

**Sergio Chirila** is married to Sharon Goodwin and is the father of Julian and Bastian. Born in the mid-70s in the Socialist Republic of Romania, he now lives in the Netherlands and works as a software engineer. He has lived and worked in Italy, Belgium, the US, and Iceland.

**Sharon Goodwin** lives in the Netherlands with her husband, who is a most amazing father, and is a stay-at-home-mom of their two sons.

**Ingrid Lundquist** is a creative spirit. After a career as a Certified Special Events Professional, she took up photography in 2011 and since then has been in more than 70 juried shows across the US and abroad. She is the founder of The Book-in-Hand Roadshow which stages presentations and workshops on topics of interest to writers. She is the author of three business books on event production, a photo story book, and two books related to self-publishing.

**Ken MacHold** followed a successful career in law enforcement by becoming a private investigator. His writings include investigative reports. He owns a small vineyard and makes his own wine. Ken is the proud winner of a bronze medal at the California State Fair in 2019 from his first harvest, a 2017 Cabernet Franc. Ken is an avid world traveler, kayaker, hiker, and skier who enjoys sharing time with his family and friends.

**Claire Manon** gained her writing experience while writing training manuals for delis and bakeries within the grocery store industry. Later, she retired from Hewlett-Packard and started a book club, which is currently in its sixteenth year. Claire volunteered for years advocating for foster youth and as a family mentor. She currently teaches culinary classes and writes short stories. She is fanatically in love with her dog, Sophie.

**Tim McCormick** is a professional sailing instructor and recovering attorney living in San Francisco. The father of three boys, his philosophy of fathering can be summed up as, "do the exact opposite of Harry Chapin's 'Cat's in the Cradle.'" In 2027 he will have no minor children for the first time in thirty-six years. Until then, he intends to go on being San Francisco's oldest and ugliest soccer mom.

**Rueben Mauricio** is a recently retired Special Education teacher of thirty-three years. He is now focusing on his next adventure, writing the libretto for his bilingual opera "Respiro / I Breathe," which takes place in 1960s Southwest Detroit and focuses on Santiago, a son of Mexican and Polish immigrants, who imagines a different life for himself.

**Margaret Teichert** steps away from the corporate world to write, travel, and make art as much as possible. She has written for business and travel publications as well as book reviews. She lives with her husband and two kids in Fair Oaks, where they can usually be found planning their next adventure.

**Cyndi Tidd** enjoys retirement and traveling to Washington and Hawaii with her husband Robert. She loves spending time with her son and his wife and every possible moment with her grandson.

**Jenyne Weingart** is a retired emergency room nurse known in the medical field for being medically intuitive. Jenyne is passionate about cooking, gardening, yoga, and quilting. Happily married for fifty-one years, she has a son, grandson, and wonderful daughter-in-law.